The Old Fashione

COTTAGES 2

Colouring Book

Compiled by Hugh Morrison

Montpelier Publishing
London
MMXV

ISBN-13:978-1522751892
ISBN-10:1522751890
Published by Montpelier Publishing, London
Printed and distributed by Amazon Createspace
This compilation © 2015

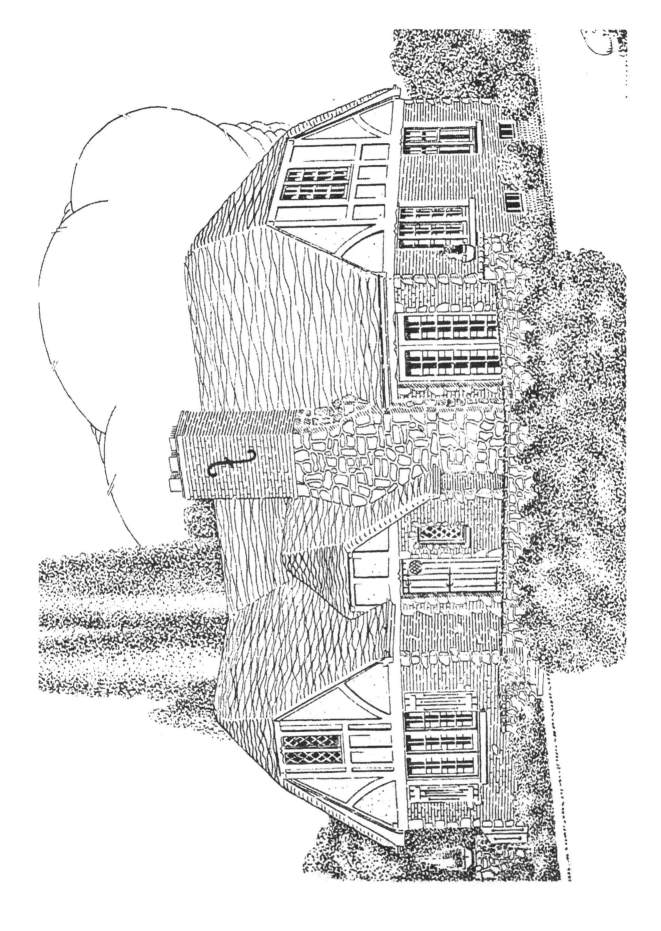

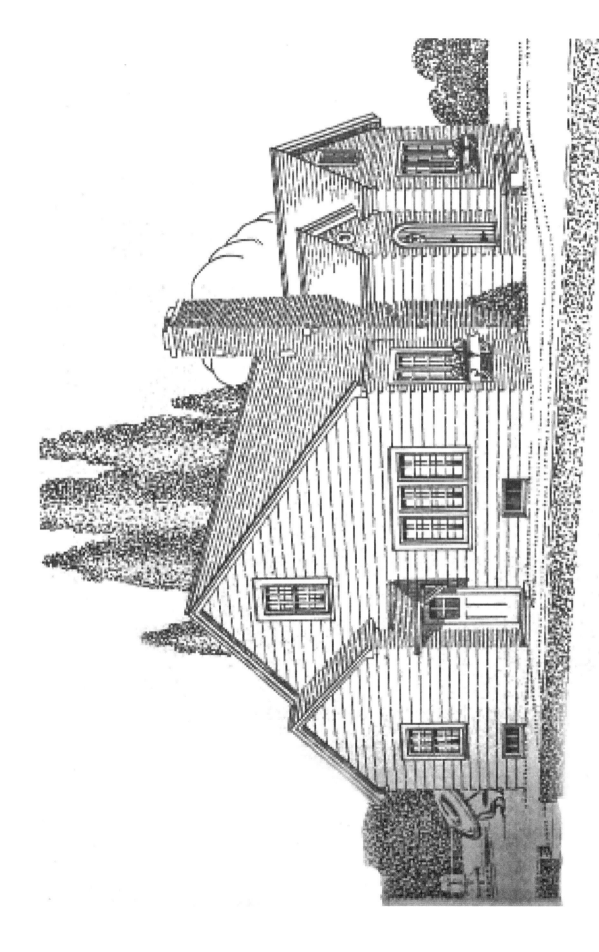

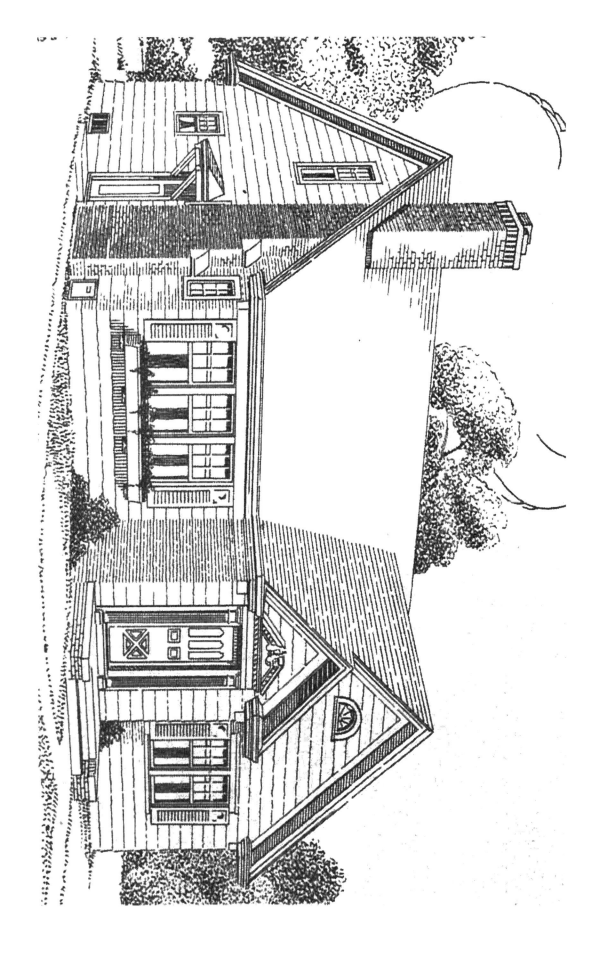

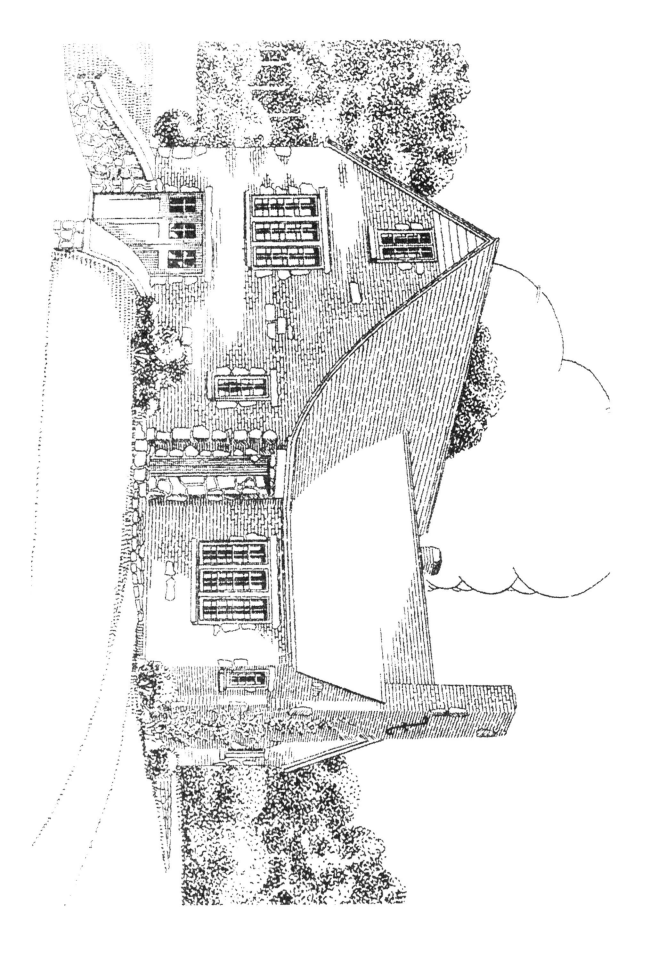

Other titles available from Montpelier Publishing

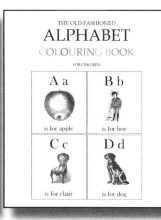

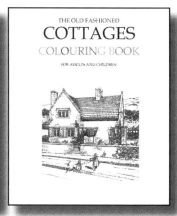

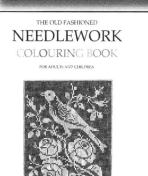

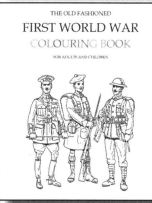

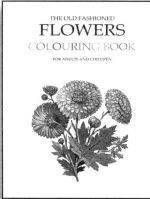

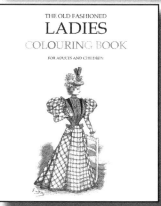

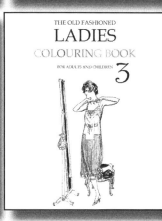

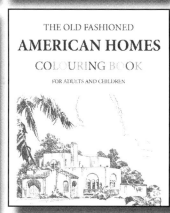

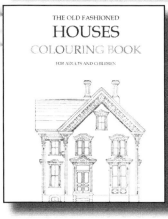

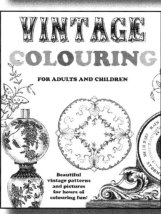

Made in the USA
Coppell, TX
23 April 2020

22126784R00017